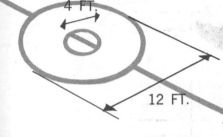

DAT

4 FT.

12 FT.

CENTER LINE

High school basketball courts are 84 ft. by 50 ft.;
college and pro courts are 94 ft. by 50 ft.

Sports Consultant:
COLONEL RED REEDER
Former Member of the West Point Coaching Staff
and Special Assistant to the West Point
Director of Athletics

THE HARLEM GLOBETROTTERS

BASKETBALL'S FUNNIEST TEAM

BY BILL GUTMAN

GARRARD PUBLISHING COMPANY
CHAMPAIGN, ILLINOIS

Library of Congress Cataloging in Publication Data

Gutman, Bill.
    The Harlem Globetrotters.

    SUMMARY: A history of the Harlem Globetrotters,
a basketball team that has successfully combined
professional ball and comedy for more than forty
years.

    1. Harlem Globetrotters—Juvenile literature.
[1. Harlem Globetrotters. 2. Basketball] I. Ti-
tle.
GV885.52.N38G87   796.32′364′0973   76-44411
ISBN 0-8116-6680-8

Photo Credits:

CBS Television: pp. 78 (bottom), 79
Children's Television Workshop: p. 78 (top)
J.R. Eyerman. Time-Life Picture Agency © Time Inc.: pp. 48,
    50 (both), 51, 52, 53
Dirck Halstead. Time Magazine © Time Inc.: pp. 72-73
New York Times Pictures: pp. 2, 26-27, 28 (top), 74, 75 (both),
    76 (both), 77 (both), jacket
Wide World Photos: p. 25
United Press International: pp. 24 (both), 28 (bottom), 29, 72

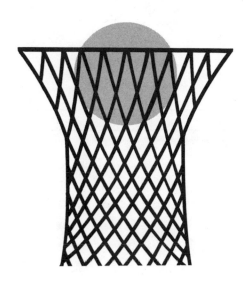

Contents

MEET
THE TROTTERS

There has never been another basketball team quite like the Harlem Globetrotters. The "Trotters," or "Globies," as they are called, play the court game in a very special way. Besides being star basketball players, the Globetrotters are also comedians. They put on a very funny show for their fans. That's what makes them different from teams like the New York Knicks, Boston Celtics, and Los Angeles Lakers.

But the Globetrotters didn't always mix basketball and comedy. They played a regular game at first. That was in 1927, when a man named Abe Saperstein decided to start his own basketball team. He wanted a team to travel around the Chicago area and play other teams. There were very few regular leagues in those days, so the Trotters played wherever they could make a few dollars. Saperstein didn't know it then, but his basketball team would go on to become the most famous in the whole world.

Basketball in the 1920s was different from today's game. There was a lot of passing and ballhandling, but not as much shooting. The scores were much lower. Sometimes just 25 or 30 points were enough to win a game. Teams rarely scored 100 or more points as they often do today. But the Trotters were a good team right from the start. They won most of their games and won them quite easily.

That was the problem. The team often played in small cities against players from those cities. Sometimes they would play the same team several times in a season. Abe Saperstein knew that if his team always won so easily, the other team wouldn't want to play them anymore. Then the Trotters would begin to lose money. So Saperstein decided to put comedy routines into the game.

Mixing comedy with serious basketball helped the Trotters do two things. First, it made the scores closer. The Trotters still won, but not by as much. Second, it made the fans laugh, and they enjoyed the game even more. It didn't take very long for the comedy routines to become a part of most Trotter games. Soon, fans came to see the fun as well as the serious basketball.

The Harlem Globetrotters have always been an all-black basketball team. When they started, blacks could only play together on their own teams. Since then, having only black players has remained part of the Trotter tradition.

The players on the Globetrotters have always worked very hard. They have to be extra good at what they do. They must master both the basketball and the comedy. They must also be ready for a long, hard season. The Trotters are always on the road. They travel many, many miles a year and play even more games than the teams in the National Basketball Association. It's a very tiring way of life. There is little chance for any rest.

At the same time, the players must always be "up." They have to be ready to smile, laugh, be funny, and entertain their many fans. So it takes a special kind of player to perform with this special kind of team.

To see how it all started, it is necessary to go back to 1927 and take a closer look at those early years, when a man named Abe Saperstein had a dream. His dream was to coach a basketball team that would travel the world.

1

THE EARLY DAYS

Abe Saperstein was born in London, England, in 1900. He was one of ten children. His father was a tailor who had to work hard to earn a living for his large family. When young Abe was just six, Mr. Saperstein brought the whole family to Chicago to look for a new and better life.

The section of Chicago where the Sapersteins lived was rough. Abe grew up a tough kid. He had to be because he was always the smallest kid around and the bigger boys sometimes picked on him. Despite his size he played basketball and baseball and also ran track at Lake View High School. He went to college for one year, but then left because he didn't have enough money and was too small to play any college sports.

That was when he became a coach and began working with kids on the Chicago playgrounds.

"It may sound corny now," Abe would say in his later years, "but I really got a kick out of helping kids. That's all I wanted to do."

So Abe Saperstein kept working with the kids on the playgrounds. He wasn't making much money, but it was the only work he enjoyed. Then, in early 1926, he met a black man named Walter Ball. Ball owned a Negro basketball team that played in the area for the Giles Post American Legion. He had decided he needed a new coach.

When he heard about Abe's fine work with youngsters, he asked Abe to coach his team. Abe jumped at the chance.

Abe was a good coach. He knew how the game should be played. He taught crisp passing, good defense, and teamwork. The Giles Post team's game improved soon after he joined it.

In November of 1926 the team had a new home and a new name. They played at a dance hall, the Savoy Ballroom. There was a basketball game before the regular dance program. So the team became the Savoy Big Five. The only trouble was that very few people came to see them play. Soon, the players became angry because they weren't making much money. Three of them walked out, and Abe Saperstein went with them. The three players were Walter "Toots" Wright, Byron "Fat" Long, and Willie "Kid" Oliver.

"It turned out to be the best break I ever got," said Abe Saperstein. "I decided then I was going to put together my own team and make money."

So Abe found two more players, Andy Washington and Bill Tupelo, to round out the starting five. Abe himself would be the only substitute. Then he needed a name for his team. It didn't take long for him to think of one. He decided to call his team the Harlem Globetrotters.

Abe's friends couldn't understand why he chose that name. Harlem was a black neighborhood in New York City. None of his players or Abe was from New York. And since the team had never been out of Chicago, how could they be called the Globetrotters?

"That's the trick," said Abe. " 'Harlem' lets people know we're a black team. And 'Harlem Globetrotters' makes it sound as if we've been around. Who knows? Maybe someday we really will travel around the world."

So on January 7, 1927, the Harlem Globetrotters played their first game. The team was supposed to be paid $25, but since the crowd was small, Abe said he'd take just $5. Five dollars for six people! Even in those days it wasn't much. Abe knew it wasn't going to be easy to make money.

"A lot of guys said the team would fold before March 1," Abe said, "but they forgot to say in what year!"

Somehow, Abe scraped together enough money to buy an old Model T Ford. The six men managed to squeeze into the car. They began to travel to all the small towns in Illinois. It was always an adventure to see if the old car would make it to the next game. The Globetrotters played any local team they could. Often their pay for an evening was less than $10. It was just about enough money to buy sandwiches and gas to get to the next game.

Basketball was a young sport then. It was played in almost any kind of building where a basket could be hung. The Globetrotters played in some very strange places in those early years.

In one place, there were big stone pillars on the floor. The players could actually hide behind them and then sneak out to shoot baskets. They also played in an opera house with a low ceiling. It was so low that at the first jump ball, the Globetrotter center bumped his head on the ceiling!

Another time they played in a drained out swimming pool. The team with the basket at the deep end had to go downhill, and the one with the basket at the shallow end had to go uphill. Another place had a red-hot, potbellied stove at each end of the floor to warm the building. The players had to be careful dribbling around it or they'd get burned.

In still another place three men wearing cowboy outfits and carrying guns came up to Saperstein before the game and told him that the local team hadn't lost in three years. They said the Trotters better not win! But they won easily, then speeded out of town as fast as the Model T could take them!

That was what basketball was like in the late 1920s. Yet the Trotters didn't quit. From January to March of 1927, the team won 63 games and lost just 12. During that summer Abe made his players work hard on all the fundamentals of the game. He was getting them ready for their first full season, the season of 1927-28. They were becoming a really good team. The starting five were all outstanding players. Abe was still the sixth man. Even though he was very short, he was a good dribbler, and whenever he played, he played well. However, he didn't play very often.

The Globetrotters traveled and played as much as they could during that first full year. They played 107 games and had an amazing record of 101 victories and only six losses. That record would make any coach happy, but not Abe Saperstein. In a way, it worried him.

"I loved to win," said Abe, "but I also knew that if we made the local team look like outclassed bums, they'd never invite us back again. Still, I couldn't ask my guys to stop playing basketball."

He also worried about the players themselves. The schedule was very hard and long. The traveling would tire any man out, and the players still weren't earning much money. When the men won so easily most of the time, there was a good chance they'd become bored. Abe felt he had to do something.

Finally, he figured out what he had to do. By early 1929 he had the player to do it. Big Inman Jackson joined the team as a center. He was a great player and also a great showman. That was the answer. To help entertain both the fans and the players, the Trotters began to put comedy routines into their easy games.

2

FROM BASKETBALL
TO
COMEDY

The comedy started slowly. The Trotters would play straight basketball at the beginning of each game. Most times they were a lot better than the team they were playing, and they'd take a big lead. Often when the game wasn't even half over, everyone already knew that the Trotters would win. Sometimes people would leave early because the game wasn't interesting anymore. But once Abe Saperstein told his team to start clowning, nobody left until the final buzzer.

It usually happened the same way every game. The Trotters would grab a big lead with their running, fast-paced style. Soon

Elmer Robinson guards Paul Arizin of Villanova as he jumps to make the shot.

Close guarding by Trotter Charles Cooper stops a shot by All-Star Gerry Calabrese.

Playing to Win:
Globetrotters vs. College All-Stars

The Globetrotters built their reputation as expert ballhandlers in contests with the College All-Stars and, later, in exhibition games with NBA teams.

J.C. Gipson sinks a basket as three All-Stars try to stop him.

All eyes are on the ball
as Elmer Robinson
takes a rebound.

Willie Gardner goes up to drop one in.

Nat Clifton displays his solid dribbling style.

Wilt Chamberlain, in his first year with the Trotters, easily shoots over his opponent's outstretched arm.

some of the players would begin looking tired from racing up and down the court. That's when Abe would give Inman Jackson a signal, and the big center would go into his routine. He would swing the ball behind his back, then roll it up and down on his arms. He never lost control. Inman could roll the ball down one arm, catch it in his large hand, then roll it back up the other arm, and pull it out from behind his head.

Since players in those days were much smaller than they are today, very few of them could "palm" the basketball. That means being able to hold the ball with one hand and swing it all around without dropping it. Jackson could do this easily with either hand, and the fans roared when he'd fake a one-handed pass and not let go of the ball.

Inman was also an expert at spinning the basketball on his fingertips. He could keep the ball going for minutes at a time, as the crowds gasped and clapped their hands. Sometimes players on the other team would try to take the ball away from Jackson as he swung it behind his back and between his legs, but they couldn't do it. During "Big Jack's" performances, the other four Trotters would sit down on the court for a rest. This made the fans laugh even more.

Before long, Inman began doing more things. Sometimes he would drive the man guarding him crazy by faking a pass one way and throwing the ball the other way. After doing this several times, he'd just keep faking, holding the ball as the man guarding him jumped from side to side.

Then, after setting his man up, Inman would place the ball on top of the man's head and simply walk away. Under the rules, that gave the ball to the other team, but the Trotters didn't care. By then they were always way ahead, and the fans loved it. Even more important, the fans remained at the game, waiting for more.

It didn't take Abe Saperstein long to see that Jackson's ballhandling magic and funny actions on the court were a big hit with the people. Soon he began getting his other players into the act.

As Inman Jackson remembered: "Abe told us to start messin' with the ball and I guess after a while we got a little crazy."

But it wasn't crazy to the fans in all the cities the Trotters visited. Quickly the word was out that the Trotters were a joy to watch, and more people came. They wanted to see their ballhandling antics. If the game was close and the Trotters played it straight, the fans were disappointed.

That didn't happen too often. In the 1928-29 season the Trotters won 145 games and lost just 13. The next season their record was 151-13, and the next 137-14. And in 1933-34, the team had a mark of 152-2. In those days all the teams tried hard to beat the Trotters. They just weren't good enough most of the time.

So the clowning continued. Before long, all the Trotters were experts at handling the ball. Many of them started doing the same tricks that Inman Jackson did so well, like passing behind their backs and spinning the ball on their fingertips.

It was the early 1930s, a time now known as the Great Depression. Jobs were hard to find. Many people were out of work and had very little money. Had it not been for their new comedy routines, the Trotters might have gone out of business, too. But with the cagey Saperstein running the show, there were still games almost every night. The team wasn't making a lot of money, but at least there was now a second car to travel in. They called it the "club car," and kept all their baggage and equipment in it.

No one complained, because there were games to be played. And the players were getting better. All of them were becoming passing experts, able to look one way and pass the ball the other way. Some of them were beginning to bounce the ball off their heads into the basket or shoot a basket by flipping the ball backward between their legs. Sometimes two of the Trotters would dazzle their opponents by whipping the ball back and forth to each other almost faster than the eye could see. Meanwhile the three other Trotters would relax on the court, sometimes getting a laugh by reading a newspaper or playing cards.

The early 1930s also saw the beginning of some of the most famous Globetrotter team routines, such as football or baseball. The

Trotters would start downcourt, suddenly stop, and line up in a football formation. One player would pass the ball center-style between his legs to the "quarterback." At the same time the other three would go out for passes, and usually one of them would catch the ball near the hoop for a layup.

The baseball routine had a pitcher, catcher, batter, and two fielders. The Trotters would throw the ball, hit it with their fists, then run around imaginary bases as their opponents tried to take the ball away from them. In these early routines, the Trotters weren't really breaking any basketball rules since they were making legal passes. The officials let them do it, especially since the crowds enjoyed it.

But the players on the other teams didn't always like it. In the middle and late 1930s, the Trotters always played several games a season against the Minnesota All-Stars, a team made up of college players from Notre Dame, the University of Minnesota, and St. Mary's College. In 1936, the All-Stars had a big center from Notre Dame, Ed "Moose" Krause, who would later become famous as a star football player. Each time the two teams met, Krause went up against the Trotters' center, Inman Jackson.

"Inman Jackson and I had some great duels," Krause remembered in later years. "I outscored Jackson a few times, but he got even on one occasion."

It was a hard-fought game. With a few minutes remaining, the Trotters finally had built up a solid lead. That's when they went into their comedy act. The All-Stars still wanted to win and continued to play hard. The Trotters had the ball, and Moose Krause was ready to guard Inman Jackson once again. But Jackson just folded his arms and stood there, as the crowd began laughing. Krause remembers what happened next.

"I couldn't figure it out," he said. "There I was, intent upon guarding Jackson, feet well spread, ready to meet him when he broke for the basket. What I didn't know was that one of the other Trotters had laid the ball on the floor between my feet. It was there all the time. And there was Inman, leisurely observing the game, and the crowd was laughing at me."

Big Moose saw red. He lost his temper and kicked the ball into the crowd. Then he dove into Jackson, and the two big men began wrestling on the floor.

"I remember Inman kept yelling, 'I didn't do it, Moose, I didn't do it," recalls Krause. "It was the most amazing and embarrassing thing that ever happened to me. Inman and I were good friends after that, and whenever I saw him he'd kid me about that game."

It was easy for a player to become angry when trying to steal the ball from the Globetrotters. The ball moved around so quickly that it was hard to follow. Opposing players would lunge for it, but get nothing but air. The ball was already on its way to somebody else.

The Trotters could handle the basketball better than any other team. Even in warmups before the games started, Jackson and his teammates would have the crowd gasping. Soon Saperstein saw that more and more people were coming early to watch the Trotters warm up. The warmups consisted of some fancy passing and shooting under the basket. But Saperstein always had an eye for giving the people what they liked. When he saw how popular the Trotters' warmups were becoming, he decided to make some changes.

He told the players to warm up at center

court instead of under the basket. The coach also put on a record of the "Beer Barrel Polka," a very fast number, for the players to use as a theme song. More people came early. The Trotters would form a circle at midcourt and begin whipping the ball around in time with the music. Fans clapped and shouted as each player took a turn doing his own kind of magic with the round ball.

The ball moved rapidly, up and down arms, behind backs, between legs. It was spun on fingers, bounced off heads and feet, palmed in midair, and always passed in an unexpected direction. The warmup lasted some five hectic minutes, and then the Trotters were ready to play.

It didn't take long for the Globetrotter warmup to become a permanent part of the team's show. It has remained a welcome sight right up to the present day, and the fans always come early to watch. The only change was the theme song. In the early 1940s, Saperstein heard a recording of "Sweet Georgia Brown," done by a man who called himself "Brother Bones," and who whistled the tune on top of a swinging, bluesy beat. The coach immediately made "Sweet Georgia Brown" the team's theme song, and it's been part of the Trotter warmup ever since.

The Trotters didn't become rich and famous during the 1930s. They still played in small towns for small amounts of money. The important thing was that they kept getting games and were traveling around. More and more people saw them, heard about them, and wanted to see them again.

There was even more comedy during this time, since that's what the people wanted to see. But in addition, the Trotters kept improving as a team.

For instance, there was a game in the early 1930s in a place called Woodfibre, Canada. The players on the other team were giving the Globetrotter players a hard time, even during the warmups. They were calling them names and saying insulting things. Some of the Trotters got angry. So did Abe Saperstein. They decided to play serious basketball all the way, and they won the game by the amazing score of 122-20. In those days very few teams ever scored 100 points in a game.

The 1930s were a time of growth for Abe Saperstein and his Harlem Globetrotters. The team was finding new fans with its new style, combining excellent basketball with some very funny comedy routines. Basketball wasn't a big sport then. It didn't have as many fans as baseball or even football. But better days lay ahead, and the Trotters would be ready for them.

3

WORLD'S CHAMPIONS

Until the mid 1930s there were just five players on the Globetrotter team. Coach Saperstein still served as a sixth man if a substitute was needed. But the five played almost every minute of every game, every night. Finally, Abe saw he had to expand, and he increased his squad to seven players. That allowed him to rotate his players and give them rests during the games. His players were good, and he didn't want them wearing out too soon.

He had seen that problem with some of his original players. They were getting older and finding it hard to stand up to the nightly grind. When a player did leave the team, Abe looked for just the right man to take his place. He wanted the best player he could get, one that would fit in with the Globetrotter style of play.

By the late 1930s, Abe had molded a whole new team. Inman Jackson was still there, the last of the old guard. The others were all newcomers. Their names were "Babe" Pressley, Harry Rusan, Bill Ford, Sonny Boswell, Bob Frazier, and Ted Strong. All were fine ballplayers. In fact, some say that Strong, who was a 220-pounder with huge hands, was one of the best basketball players in history.

In 1939, the team traveled to Mexico for a series of games. The tour didn't make a great deal of money for the Trotters, but many people came to see them play. And traveling out of the country gave Saperstein a chance to tell people that his team actually did go "globetrotting." Then, in early 1940, came an event which really put the Trotters on the map.

Some newspaper people in Chicago, at the *Herald-American*, decided to hold a big basketball tournament in the Windy City. They invited the finest teams from the various leagues around the country, as well as some of the best independent teams. The team that won the tournament would be declared "World Champions!"

It was a gala basketball event, maybe the biggest ever at that time. The teams invited had some strange sounding names, but they were the top basketball clubs of the day. Among them were the Waterloo Wonders, Clarksburg Oilers, Sheboygan Redskins, Oshkosh Stars, House of David, and Kenosha

Royals. The teams came from many states—Iowa, West Virginia, Indiana, Michigan, and Wisconsin—as well as from the big cities of Chicago, Washington, and New York.

When one more team was needed to fill out the field of fourteen, the Globetrotters were invited to play. Many people thought of the Trotters as clowns and comedians, not as real basketball players. They didn't think Saperstein's club had a chance against some of the better-known teams.

But the Trotters came to Chicago in a very serious mood. They wanted to prove they were good basketball players, as good as anyone else. They also wanted a chance at the $1,000 in prize money the winners would receive. A thousand dollars doesn't sound like much money today, not when the winning team in the NBA play-offs gets about $25,000 per man. But in 1940, $1,000 for the whole team was a lot. In addition, the winning team would also get a chance to play against a team of college all-stars in November.

The Trotters took to the court for their first game in the tourney on March 17, 1940. They were up against the Kenosha Royals, and everyone was asking the same questions.

"Do you think the Trotters can win?"

"Did they just come to clown around and be funny?"

But there was no laughing that night. The Trotters played straight basketball and blew the Royals right off the court, 50-26. They surprised everyone. No one thought they'd be that good. But now they had to play the New York Renaissance Five, another all-black team, which many people thought would win the tournament.

Many people say that the Globetrotter-Rens game was one of the greatest games ever

Clowns
of the Court

In the fifties the Globetrotters became famous as funnymen as well as ballplayers. The greatest comedian of them all was Goose Tatum (left), who kept audiences roaring the world over.

Some of Goose's rib-tickling routines:
he leans back on his bewildered opponent, fits a
pair of borrowed glasses on the referee, and
dunks the ball with a little help from a friend!

The ball went thataway! But who is that strange looking player at courtside?

The ball goes halfway to the basket on a rubber
band—and then snaps back!

played. The score wasn't high by today's standards, but the players showed a lot of skill. Both clubs were fast, had great ball-handlers, and played excellent defense. It was close all the way. The Rens held a one point lead, 36-35, with less than a minute to go. Then the Trotters' Sonny Boswell was fouled on a drive. He calmly made both free throws, and the Trotters held on to win, 37-36. Now they were in the semi-finals.

Once more the Trotters weren't expected to win. But this game was easier for them. They whipped the Syracuse Reds, 34-24, to move into the finals against the hometown team, the Chicago Bruins.

The Trotters also came from Chicago. But they were always on the road, and many Chicagoans didn't even know them. Most fans were rooting for the Bruins to win.

It was an exciting game from start to

finish. For most of the first half and into the third period, the Trotters were in control. They held a 20-13 lead.

Then the Bruins got hot and began hitting on every kind of shot they took. From the middle of the third period and right into the fourth, the Bruins caught and passed the Trotters. In that time they outscored the Trotters by 16-1. The fans were shouting encouragement to the favored Bruins. It looked as if the Trotters would finally fold. With just five minutes to go in the game, the Bruins held a 29-21 lead.

But then Coach Saperstein called a timeout. He talked to his team quickly and firmly. When the Trotters returned to the court, the tempo of the game changed again. The Trotters began to rally. Suddenly their shots began dropping once more. At the other end of the court, the Trotter defense was stopping the Bruins cold.

In those final five minutes the Trotters ran off 10 straight points while holding the Bruins scoreless. That gave them a 31-29 lead. Then their defense went to work and held the lead at that score. The Trotters had won the World's Championship. They had done it the hard way, coming from behind. Even when the Bruins had tried to stall and freeze the ball, the Trotter defense had taken it away from them. Suddenly basketball fans everywhere knew the names of Bernie Price, Sonny Boswell, Ted Strong, Babe Pressley, and Inman Jackson, the five Trotters who saw most of the action in the tourney.

Before the day ended, Coach Saperstein had new jackets delivered to his team. On the back of each were the words: WORLD'S CHAMPIONS. The Trotters had arrived.

Things were really looking up for the Trotters now. That November, as winners of the tourney, they met a strong squad of college all-stars. The game was played in Chicago before a crowd of nearly 22,000 fans.

It was an exciting, hair-raising game from start to finish. It was close all the way. When the regular time ran out, the game was tied, and the two teams went into overtime. Finally, the All-Stars managed a close, 44-42, victory. Even though the Trotters lost, it was that game that really brought them new fans.

Abe Saperstein often said: "That was the night we came into our own, the night we won a million followers and really started going places. The fact that we almost beat one of the greatest collections of basketball talent ever gathered on one floor proved to the public that there was such a team as the Globetrotters and that it was not only good, but a crowd pleaser."

It may be difficult for fans of today's basketball to understand why these low-scoring games were so exciting. One long-time basketball writer, Leo Fischer, who has watched basketball grow with the years, said it this way:

"Let me tell you that the modern fan doesn't get to see too much of the expert ball-handling, the maneuvering, the faking, the teamwork that characterized the sport in that era.... In that period, when you made a basket, you earned it—and that meant something, too."

The Trotters had proved to the basketball world that they could play the game and play it well.

In the years that followed, the Trotters would prove their skills over and over again, usually in games against college all-star teams, but also against teams from the new National Basketball Association.

But it wasn't their playing skill that would bring them to new heights of popularity in the coming years. It was their other talent, their clowning, that brought the people out to see the Trotters. In the season following the tournament victory and the close loss to the All-Stars, the Trotters found a player who would lead them into this new era.

4

GOOSE TATUM TAKES CHARGE

His name was Reece Tatum, but everyone called him by his nickname—Goose. It was a nickname he got in his hometown of El Dorado, Arkansas. The story was that when he played touch football with his friends, Tatum could outleap anyone to catch passes. One day he went way up in the air for one and a friend remarked, "Look at that ol' Goose fly!"

From that day on he was "Goose" Tatum. Abe Saperstein first saw him in 1941, when Tatum was playing, of all things, baseball. He was a first baseman with the Cincinnati Clowns, a team in the old Negro leagues. Goose wasn't a great hitter, but he loved to clown around. Saperstein saw something in Goose and knew he could make him into a star basketball player. The clowning just came naturally.

Goose Tatum was perfectly built for the part he was to play. He stood six feet, three inches tall, and had long arms which dangled almost to his knees. He also had huge hands which enabled him to handle a basketball as if it were a baseball. In addition, he had a very expressive face with large eyes and mouth. These features let him show any emotion to the fans in seconds.

Some of the older players didn't really understand why Saperstein brought Tatum to the Trotters in 1941. They didn't think he had played enough basketball before, and they didn't know what his role with the team would be. There might have been some trouble over this had it not been for World War II, which the United States entered in December 1941. Tatum, like so many other athletes, went into the army and was gone for nearly four years. During that time Abe kept the team together, though he didn't have the players he really wanted. He was forced to use older players and youngsters who weren't ready. But with the war always in the news, people needed an occasional laugh, and they kept coming to see the Trotters play.

When the war ended in 1945, the Trotters were ready to grow again. Tatum had played a great deal of basketball while in the army and returned a much better player. Now Abe knew what he'd do. He'd build a new ten-man team around Reece "Goose" Tatum.

The combination clicked like magic. With the hilarious Tatum leading the way, the Trotters began playing to larger and larger crowds in big arenas. By 1947, they were selling out the house everywhere they went. People were beginning to call them the number one attraction in all of sport. After 20 years of hard work, travel, and sweat, the Harlem Globetrotters were finally making it big.

Saperstein was finding other outstanding players to go along with Tatum. Marques Haynes was one. His specialty was dribbling the ball, and he was accurately billed as the "World's Greatest Dribbler." Haynes could dribble the basketball in any position—standing, sitting, kneeling, even lying down. He could dribble with either hand and dribble so low that the ball wouldn't come more than an inch off the floor.

Haynes's dribbling soon became part of

every Globetrotter game. At some point in the action, the other four Trotters would sit down on the court and let Marques take over. He'd go into his act, keeping the ball away from the five players on the other team—simply by dribbling. His opponents would dive at the ball, try to corner him, even bump him, but they couldn't take the ball away. Even after Haynes left the team, the Trotters always had a dribbling star in the tradition of Marques Haynes.

Tatum and Haynes were the two best-known Trotters in the 1940s and 1950s. But there were other greats too, such as Nat "Sweetwater" Clifton, who was later to become one of the first two black players in the National Basketball Association. Leon Hillard was another long-time Trotter standout. He had an electrifying two-hand set shot from way out, and later took over from Haynes as the team's dribbling star.

But to many, it was the clowning of Goose Tatum that put the team in the big time.

As one writer said: "Goose Tatum was a remarkable clown. He knew just when the crowd wanted entertainment and when it wanted basketball."

It was Goose Tatum more than any other man who gave the Trotters the style and comedy routines the team still uses today. Even the team offense was more suited to Tatum and his comedy than to straight basketball. Goose would often stand in the pivot, and the other players would keep throwing the ball to him. Then it was up to him to play it his way. He could throw it back to a teammate or begin doing tricks with it, like spinning it on his finger, swinging it behind his back and between his legs, or bouncing it off his head or foot.

The players guarding Tatum would go

crazy trying to keep up with him. Sometimes they couldn't even follow the ball. Goose would put it between their legs on the floor, and they wouldn't know it was there. Then he'd run around behind them, pick it up again, and score if he wanted to.

It was also Tatum who signaled when the team was ready to try for a basket. Sometimes Goose would go for it himself. He could drive to the hoop or take a hook shot. Or he could pass the ball and let someone else take the shot.

While the team was still beating almost every club it played, Goose was making the comedy routines funnier and funnier. He started by making some of the older routines even better. People laughed harder at the baseball and football routines once Goose took over. Tatum was also the first Globetrotter to use the audience in his comedy routines.

Sometimes Goose would just stroll into the stands and sit down on a fan's lap. Other times he'd borrow a hat he liked from a fan, come back, and play with it on for a while. If there was a photographer at courtside or a fan with a camera, Goose would stop playing and pose for a picture. When a foul was called on Goose, he'd often go into the stands, borrow a pair of eyeglasses from a fan, and give them to the referee.

Goose also started some other routines. One was a mock chase through the stands with a water bucket. When Goose finally dumped the bucket, tiny pieces of paper poured out instead of water. The fans loved that because they had thought they might be drenched.

Goose was always up to something. When there was a timeout, he'd tip-toe to the other team's huddle and listen to what they were saying. Then his face would break out in a huge grin, and he'd run back to his own team's huddle to report on what was happening.

Once a game, Goose would go down hard after a foul and pretend he couldn't continue. He'd be helped to the sideline, limping badly. Then he'd make a sudden recovery and return to take his foul shot. Goose would wind up and shoot. Players from both sides would jump in the lane for a rebound. But the ball would suddenly be right back in Goose's hands while he shrieked with laughter. Goose had switched balls. He now had one with a rubber band that snapped back to him after going halfway to the basket. That was one of the Trotters' favorites.

It seemed as if the Trotters were always doing something with the ball. If it wasn't being passed around at a magical rate, it was hidden under someone's shirt, or being switched for the rubber-band ball. Another routine was to substitute a ball that wouldn't bounce right or wouldn't bounce at all. The other team always got that one.

There was still another routine in which the Trotters literally ate the ball. They had a special ball made of bread, which they'd suddenly break apart and begin eating, as the crowd roared with laughter once again.

Most of the laughter was Goose's doing. Most people agreed that Goose was a comic genius. One writer, Marshall Smith, said that, "with a few simple changes in techniques and trappings, he could take his place among the funnymen in the Ringling big top and find himself playing to an easy-laughing house."

Abe Saperstein, who perhaps knew Goose best, said this about the Trotters' chief funnyman: "A lot of people try to be funny, but they fall flat on their faces because they lack that sixth sense that tells a genius like Tatum precisely the time to punch across a particular caper."

Goose sometimes worried Abe, though. He liked to disappear every once in a while and wander around on his own. But he usually showed up in time for the game. In fact, it was sometimes hard to keep him away. He once played with a dangerously high fever, and another time with a severe back injury. Saperstein always marveled at Goose's courage.

"That man is a contradiction," Abe would say. "He'll worry you half to death sometimes over little things. But he'd rather risk his health than endanger the show."

With Goose Tatum leading the way, the Trotters became more popular than ever in the late 1940s. In fact, they were probably the most popular basketball team in the

On a visit to the White House, Curly Neal shows President Ford some expert ballhandling.

Playing in Helsinki, Finland, Meadowlark Lemon flies through the air on a jump shot.

Doing It Their Way:
The Globetrotters Today

Great basketball and comedy too—that's the Harlem
Globetrotter style today. In this country and abroad,
on the road and on television, the Trotters combine
both in an act that delights their audiences.

Pablo Robertson (above) and Frank Streety (top right) use their dribbling talents to hang on to the ball.

Finger magic helps Meadowlark Lemon (bottom right) pass the ball.

Bobby Hunter "drenches" the audience with a bucketful of confetti.

Meadowlark Lemon performs a little sleight-of-hand with the ball.

A piggy-back riding player on the opposing team gets into the act!

**The Trotters talk things over—
in a football huddle!**

The Trotters, television
stars of the seventies: on
"Sesame Street" (above);
comedian Bill Cosby and
Trotter Bobby Hunter as
detectives on "The Harlem
Globetrotters' Popcorn
Machine" (right)

The Globetrotters swing into a song and dance routine with singer Teresa Graves on "The Harlem Globetrotters' Popcorn Machine."

country. In those days, the National Basketball Association was just beginning, and the crowds didn't always come to the NBA games. Yet the Trotters could almost fill any arena in any city. So the NBA people often asked the Trotters to play the first game of a doubleheader, with two NBA teams in the second game. Saperstein usually agreed. That brought the fans out to see the Trotters, and most of them stayed for the NBA game. In this way the Trotters helped to start the NBA, even though there were no black players in the NBA at the time.

As the Trotters' reputation as clowns spread even further, people again began saying that they couldn't play real basketball. Abe and his players never liked this charge, so during the 1948 basketball season they arranged a game with the best team in the NBA, the Minneapolis Lakers.

The Lakers were a great team then, the NBA's best. They had the first of the big supercenters in six feet, ten inch George Mikan, and other fine players such as Jim Pollard, Slater Martin, and Vern Mikkelsen. Not too many people thought the Trotters could win.

But they did. Once again the Trotters set the basketball world upside down. In a close, hard-fought game, they beat the champion Lakers by two points, 61-59. The Lakers had height, but they couldn't keep up with the Trotters' speed and ball-handling.

The funny men of basketball were still among the best players in the world. The Trotters played the Lakers the following year and beat them once again. Then, in 1950, the Trotters began another series that lasted for twelve years.

It was known as the "World Series of

Basketball". It was a series of games between the Trotters and a team of college all-stars, which generally had the best college seniors in the country. Some of the great collegians and later pros who played for the All-Stars were Bob Cousy, Paul Arizin, Cliff Hagen, Frank Ramsey, Bob Leonard, Frank Selvy, Gene Shue, Larry Costello, Tom Gola, Bill Sharman, Tom Heinsohn, Jack Twyman, Walt Bellamy, K.C. Jones, Guy Rodgers, Tom Merschery, and Larry Siegfried. All of these men went on to long careers in the NBA.

Yet the Trotters always won more than they lost. The first year, 1950, the Trotters beat the All-Stars 11 out of 18 times. From 1950 to 1962, the Trotters won 146 games and lost just 66 to the All-Stars. The Trotters won the series each year, and in 1962, the last year it was played, the Trotters won 15 of 16 games.

By 1962 basketball had changed. The National Basketball Association was on solid ground and had most of the great players, including many black stars. They had been coming in steadily since the mid 1950s. In a sense, the NBA didn't need the Trotters anymore to boost the crowds.

And the Trotters no longer needed to prove their skills against the College All-Stars. Trotter fans wanted comedy. The team was booked solid because so many people wanted to see their special kind of basketball.

So after 1962, the Harlem Globetrotters never played serious, competitive basketball again. All of those zany routines, perfected by Abe Saperstein, Inman Jackson, Goose Tatum, and others, were what the people paid to see.

5

TODAY'S TROTTERS

By the 1960s, the whole world knew about the Harlem Globetrotters. In fact, the Trotters were usually entertaining people in one corner of the world or another. The team made its first trip overseas in 1950 and has been going abroad every year since. It has performed in more than 90 countries throughout the world.

So great was the Trotters' success that in recent years the club has divided into two teams. One travels around the United

States, while the other fills requests from all over the world.

Abe Saperstein remained as owner and coach of the team until his death in 1966. Since then, a new group of people has run the Trotters. There is also a new group of players, who do many of the same tricks that the Trotters have been doing for years. Nowadays, instead of playing a variety of "serious teams," the Trotters play the same team every night. That team is there simply to let the Trotters put on their show.

In the early 1970s, a man named Meadowlark Lemon (his real name) was the chief clown of the Trotters. Meadowlark played the same role that Goose Tatum had played for so long. Other top players for the Trotters of the seventies were Curly Neal, Geese Ausbie, and Theodis Lee. After some years away from the team, the great Marques Haynes returned in the early seventies to once again show fans his great dribbling act.

Other famous athletes have played with the Trotters. Both Wilt Chamberlain and Connie Hawkins, great NBA players, were regulars with the team for a while. St. Louis Cardinals pitcher Bob Gibson also played with the team at one time. Another great baseball pitcher, Ferguson Jenkins, enjoys playing with the Trotters whenever he can, as does ex-boxer Suger Ray Robinson.

To men like Ferguson Jenkins and Sugar Ray, the Trotters are pure fun, and that's the way most people see them. The team continues to make the fans laugh, even though some people have begun to criticize it for not changing its routines. Others have come to the team's defense.

"Watching the Trotters is like watching a rerun of a favorite movie," one sportswriter has written. "You know what's going to happen, but it hardly matters because the entertainment factor is never dulled."

There have been other criticisms of the team in recent years. Some people have said the time has come for the Trotters to have white players on the team. Perhaps they will someday. But the Trotters are a team deep in tradition, and part of that tradition is to be an all-black team.

What's it like to be a Harlem Globetrotter? It's a difficult job. There are games almost every night. The Trotters play more games each year than teams in the NBA.

There are hours spent on the bus and more hours in a hotel room, just waiting for the game that night. But no matter how a player feels, he has to look sharp on the court. He must step lively, smile, grin, chatter, and make it seem as though each game is the first he's played in a week.

Many players have left the team over the years because they must travel so much of the time. Then the team must find new players. Scouts are continually looking for players all over the country. Each year some 30 men are invited to the Trotters' training camp.

The training camp is hard on young players. They have a week to show what they can do. Then the coaching staff cuts about 20 of them. The ones that are left continue to work out with the regular Trotter team.

For two weeks the team works out twice a day. The players work to get in top physical shape, and also to improve their shooting, speed, and ballhandling. In the end, only 20 players will remain, 10 on each of the Trotters' two units. So there may be room for only one or two rookies.

It's very difficult for a youngster to make the team. He must be talented and work very, very hard, And he has to be able to play the Globetrotter style of basketball. Once the teams have been selected, the Trotters go on the road, and rookies, as well as veterans, begin to feel the grind.

When the Trotters come to town they do it with flare. Even if the game is to be played in a small town, rather than in a large city, everyone knows the Trotters are on their way.

Many times the team sends former players to a town ahead of time. They go to sportswriters, talk on the radio, and appear on television to tell everyone the Trotters are coming. The home office in Chicago sends out press releases about the history of the Globetrotters. There are Globetrotter quizzes and Globetrotter basketball tips —anything to keep the team in the news until game time. By then the game is usually sold out.

The Trotters like everyone to come out, young and old, men and women. They bill their show as the "world's greatest family entertainment."

Then comes game day. The players sometimes arrive early to mingle with the crowds and sign autographs. They play their game, stay late to sign autographs again, then head back for the bus, and go on to the next town. When they leave, there's usually a lot of goodwill remaining behind.

Once, after the Trotters had left a small midwestern town, a sports reporter wrote: "If you would ask any of the fans what the final scores were, you probably would receive a blank stare. 'Who cares,' they'd say. 'We just had a lot of fun!'"

In another small town a sports editor wrote, "[The Trotters] proved they're champion human beings, too. They roamed the grandstand area, talking with kids, signing autographs, posing for pictures, doing anything they were asked to do."

Because so many of the cities on the United States tour are close together, the Trotters travel by bus, not by airplane. Their bus is very special. It has comfortable seats, which drop back so the players can sleep. There is also a bathroom on the bus, a refrigerator, television, special card tables, and a very good stereo system.

The players do different things on the bus. Some like to sleep, so they'll be well rested for the next game. Others play cards, continuing their games from city to city. Geese Ausbie liked to pass the time writing letters to everyone he knew, while Curly Neal drew sketches of the passing countryside.

Some of the players just read, everything from magazines and newspapers to serious novels. Others listen to music on their own tape recorders, while a few men play chess, and still others watch television. Marques Haynes, who traveled with the Trotters for so many years, usually just relaxed and stared out at the scenery. Each player must find the best way to spend his time on the bus.

Besides putting on their show, the Trotters also find time to help young people. They conduct basketball clinics in many cities. They teach youngsters how to play the game as well as how to perform many of their famous ballhandling tricks. If anyone loves the Harlem Globetrotters, it's the kids.

In the 1970s, the Trotters were on television more than ever before. They often appeared on "Sesame Street," an educational show for children. They also had two children's shows of their own.

One was a cartoon show called "The

Harlem Globetrotters," with all the Trotter players pictured as animated cartoon characters. The other show was "The Harlem Globetrotters' Popcorn Machine," in which all the real players appeared in comedy sketches, songs, and dances. The show also included some of the Trotters' great basketball routines. The "Popcorn Machine" was funny, but the Trotters hoped it would also set a good example for youngsters and help them to learn.

Besides working with youngsters, the Trotters have made millions of people forget their problems with laughter. They have also played benefit games to earn money for good causes.

"Sesame Street" and "Popcorn Machine" were not the Trotters' first appearances on television. The team first entertained on TV in 1954 on the old "Ed Sullivan Show." Since then, they have appeared countless times. Sometimes their games have been shown. Other times they've just done their famous warmup routine to "Sweet Georgia Brown."

So the Trotters today are more popular than ever before. It's still important for people to laugh, and in that department the Trotters are hard to beat.

They continue to use their old routines and are looked upon now primarily as comedians, especially by those who don't know about the Trotters' important role in the history of basketball. Those who remember the early days, however, usually agree with Meadowlark Lemon.

"The Globetrotters made it possible for blacks to play basketball when nobody would give them a chance," the famous player has often said. "We kept the NBA alive in the early days playing double-headers with them. The same with the

95

ABA. There is nothing wrong with combining basketball and comedy."

Meadowlark Lemon is right. The Harlem Globetrotters have made a tremendous contribution to basketball, while at the same time bringing laughter and happiness to fans everywhere. They have always done it their way, and they have been doing it with greater success than any team in the history of sport.

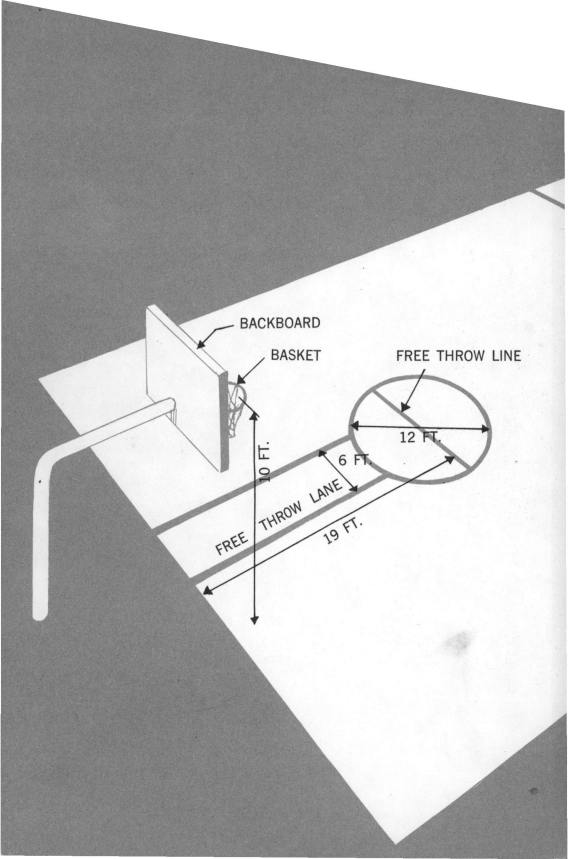

BACKBOARD

BASKET

FREE THROW LINE

12 FT.

6 FT.

10 FT.

FREE THROW LANE

19 FT.